TRACING
Genesis Curriculum
The Book of Genesis

2019 Edition

This workbook belongs to

_____

 # Day 1

Color the day number if you like. Trace and write today's spelling words.

formless _____

void _____

darkness _____

moving _____

_____

_____

_____

_____

Color in today's vocabulary word. Draw a picture to show its meaning. It means completely empty or a completely empty space. Here are some sentences that use the word.

It sounded like someone answered the phone, but no one spoke. It was just void on the other end of the line.

If you feel a void in your heart, you can ask Jesus to fill it with His Spirit.

Day 2

Trace and then write today's words.

dry

expanse

separate

seas

Color in today's vocabulary word. Draw a picture to show its meaning. It means a large open area. Here are some sentences that use the word.

I love seeing the sunrise over the vast expanse of ocean.

The fluffy clouds filled the expanse of the blue sky.

Day 3

Trace and then write today's words.

brought _____

vegetation _____

yield _____

bearing _____

_____

_____

_____

_____

Color in today's vocabulary word. Draw a picture to show its meaning. It means to produce. Here are some sentences that use the word.

With all of the rain this season, we yielded our best tomato crop this year.

How many cookies does this recipe say it will yield?

Day 4

Trace and then write today's words.

light _____

heaven _____

sign _____

season _____

_____

_____

_____

_____

govern

Color in today's vocabulary word. Draw a picture to show its meaning. It means to rule, or to be in be in control over a group of people. Here are some sentences that use the word.

He governed over his country with wisdom.

She built a fort out of pillows and blankets and governed over her kingdom of stuffed animals.

Day 5

Trace and then write today's words.

In the beginning God
created the heavens
and the earth.

Draw a picture of a bird. Make sure to show those features which make birds birds!

Day 6

Trace and then write today's words.

fruitful _____

multiply _____

fifth _____

which _____

_____

_____

_____

_____

swarm

Color in today's vocabulary word. Draw a picture to show its meaning. It means to abound, to teem, or to be overrun. Here are some sentences that use the word.

The bees swarmed towards me after I accidently disturbed their hive.

Swarms of people are expected to show up for the concert tonight.

Day 7

Trace and then write today's words.

creature

beast

ground

kind

Color in today's vocabulary word. Draw a picture to show its meaning. It means to move slowly and carefully, especially to avoid notice. Here are some sentences that use the word.

The creeping mouse hoped he wouldn't be caught.

He decided to creep into the room to surprise her.

Day 8

Trace and then write today's words.

rule _____

image _____

likeness _____

over _____

_____

_____

_____

dimension

Color in today's vocabulary word. Draw a picture to show its meaning. It means measurement, or an aspect of something. Here are some sentences that use the word.

Measure the dimensions of the room so that we can figure out how much paint we need.

This is a more complicated project than I thought; there are many dimensions to it.

Day 9

Trace and then write today's words.

subdue _____

surface _____

earth _____

sky _____

_____

_____

_____

_____

Color in today's vocabulary word. Draw a picture to show its meaning. It means to bring under control. Here are some sentences that use the word.

The ruler subdued his people with a promise to provide everyone with bread.

He subdued the vicious dog by tossing him some meat.

Day 10

Trace and then write today's words.

Let everything that has breath praise the Lord.

_____

_____

_____

_____

Today's science lesson is about orbits. The earth orbits the sun and the moon orbits the earth. Can you draw a picture of it?

Day 11

Trace and then write today's words.

shrub _____

sprouted _____

creation _____

mist _____

_____

_____

_____

_____

Color in today's vocabulary word. Draw a picture to show its meaning. It means a cloud of tiny water droplets near the earth's surface. Here are some sentences that use the word.

When I woke up this morning, the mist was visible out my window.

At the grocery store, they shoot out a cool mist of water over the vegetables to keep them fresh.

Day 12

Trace and then write today's words.

breathed

breath

nostrils

being

Color in today's vocabulary word. Draw a picture to show its meaning. It means in the middle of. Here are some sentences that use the word.

I was lost in the midst of the crowd.

It was sad to see trash in the midst of the beautiful surroundings.

Day 13

Trace and then write today's words.

third

fourth

flows

river

Color in today's vocabulary word. Draw a picture to show its meaning. It means to separate into parts. Here are some sentences that use the word.

We divided into teams to play.

We divided up the chores and got our work done quickly that way.

Day 14

Trace and then write today's words.

cultivate _____

garden _____

Eden _____

continent _____

_____

_____

_____

_____

Color in today's vocabulary word. Draw a picture to show its meaning. It means to prepare and use land for crops or to develop. Here are some sentences that use the word.

She cultivated the land and was able to provide her family with fresh vegetables.

He cultivated gratefulness in his life and was always quick to say thank you.

Day 15

Trace and then write today's memory verse words.

The Spirit of God was
moving over the
surface of the waters.

_____

_____

_____

_____

_____

circulatory system

Color in today's words. Your science lesson the other day was on the circulatory system, your body system that pumps and carries blood through your body. Can you draw a diagram of it?

Day 16

Trace and then write today's words.

reason _____

join _____

slept _____

ashamed _____

_____

_____

_____

fashion

Color in today's vocabulary word. Draw a picture to show its meaning. It means to take materials and to make them into something. Here are some sentences that use the word.

God fashioned Eve from one of Adam's rib bones.

My grandfather could fashion a chair out of any old materials around the house.

Day 17

Trace and then write today's words.

sewed

themselves

touch

coverings

Color in today's vocabulary word. Draw a picture to show its meaning. It means clever at using deception to get what you want. Here are some sentences that use the word.

Satan was crafty in getting Eve to take the forbidden fruit.

The little boy was crafty in sneaking a cookie from the kitchen.

Day 18

Trace and then write today's words.

presence

enmity

whistle

bruise

Color in today's vocabulary word. Draw a picture to show its meaning. It means hatred. Here are some sentences that use the word.

There was enmity between them ever since their disagreement.

There is enmity between me and the rat hiding in that hole.

Day 19

Trace and then write today's words.

stationed

guard

direction

flaming

Color in today's vocabulary word. Draw a picture to show its meaning. It means to put someone in position in a particular place for a particular purpose. Here are some sentences that use the word.

I was stationed by the door to greet people.

He was stationed at the drink table to help serve people the lemonade.

 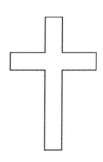

Trace and then write today's memory verse words.

For all have sinned and
fall short of the glory
of God.

_____

_____

_____

_____

Color in today's words. Today's science lesson is on the desert. Can you draw a desert plant or animal?

Day 21

Trace and then write today's words.

Cain _____

wanderer _____

field _____

blood _____

_____

_____

_____

_____

brother's keeper

Color in today's vocabulary word. Draw a picture to show its meaning. It means to be in charge of someone else or to look after them.

Some think we are to be our brother's keeper and help them when they are in trouble.

Some think we shouldn't be our brother's keeper and should not try to control the actions of others.

Day 22

Trace and then write today's words.

great

driven

vagrant

vengeance

vagrant

Color in today's vocabulary word. Draw a picture to show its meaning. It means a wanderer and someone who begs for a living. Here are some sentences that use the word.

There was a vagrant panhandling on the street corner.

He became a vagrant after he lost his job, home, and family.

Day 23

Trace and then write today's words.

father

dwell

tents

birth

presence

Color in today's vocabulary word. Draw a picture to show its meaning. It means to being there, whether seen or not. Here are some sentences that use the word.

His presence was felt by everyone in the room.

Our group made its presence known by our loud cheering.

Day 24

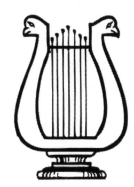

Trace and then write today's words.

lyre

implements

speech

striking

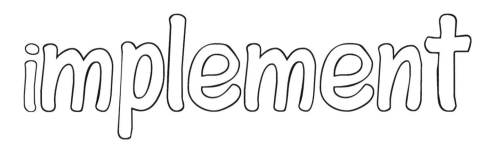

Color in today's vocabulary word. Draw a picture to show its meaning. An implement is a tool made for a particular use, or it can mean to put a plan into action. Here are some sentences that use the word.

We need some sort of cutting implement to open this.

Will you implement this design when you build your home?

Day 25

Trace and then write today's words.

No temptation has
overtaken you but
such as is common to
man.

solar system

Today's science lesson is about the solar system. Draw a solar system, rocks (that includes planets and moons) orbiting a star.

Day 26

The first and last letters of these words have been switched. Can you write the real words?

tidsm __ __ __ __ __

ightl __ __ __ __ __ __

govinm __ __ __ __ __ __ __

neasos __ __ __ __ __ __

 Day 27

Fill in the missing letters and then put those letters into the puzzle below.

m i d __ __
1   2

This word means a large open area.

 expan__e
1

This word means to divide into parts.

separa__e
2

Day 28

Can you find these words in the puzzle?

earth, sky, shrub, ground

They are written across like regular words and are in all caps letters like this: EARTH, SKY, SHRUB, GROUND.

```
V P W F P B
S O A U T A
G R O U N D
E A R T H T
V V Z S K Y
S H R U B H
```

The beginnings and ends of the words have been mixed up. Can you put the words back in order? Cut out the word parts and rearrange them or write the real words on the lines. (Parent note: If you want to cut these out but not cut your book, come to genesiscurriculum.com to print this page.)

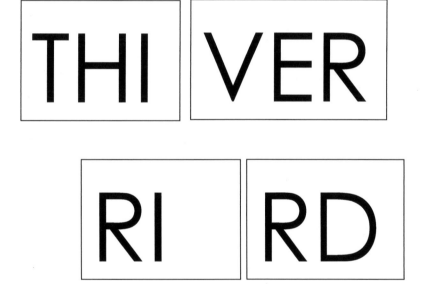

_____

_____

Can you fill in the puzzle with these words? guard flaming bruise

Today you're going to draw a line through some nouns. Every time you read a word that's a person, draw a line through it. Choose a light color so you can still see the word. A person might be a name, like Rachel, or it might be a person like the mayor or even just a boy. Is a boy a person? Yes! Give it a try. It's okay if you miss one. (A little note: Don't put a line through the word "he" even though that is referring to a person.)

A boy named Tom rode his bike down the street toward the school. He waved to his neighbor to say hello. His neighbor worked at Walmart but was home today. Then he saw the mailman coming. He raced home and asked his mom if he could wait by the mailbox.

Can you match the words to their definitions? Draw a line between each word and its meaning.

govern   a large, wide, open area

expanse   to move slowly to avoid notice

crafty   a tool

midst   to rule

implement   in the middle of

creep   clever at using deception

Day 33

Today you're going to draw a line through some more nouns. This time, every time you read a word that's a place, draw a line through it. Choose a light color so you can still see the word. A place might be something like the store, or it might be the name of a place like California or Home Depot. Give it a try. It's okay if you miss one. It's also okay if you want to mark people again. We're finding nouns and those are nouns.

A boy named Tom rode his bike down the street toward the school. He waved to his neighbor to say hello. His neighbor worked at Walmart but was home today. Then he saw the mailman coming. He raced home and asked his mom if he could wait by the mailbox.

Day 34

Can you use the definitions to write in the words? This is a trickier one. You can use the vocabulary word pages in this book and the puzzle from Day 32 to help you.

1. in the middle of 2. a large, wide open area 3. clever at using deception
4. completely empty 5. to rule

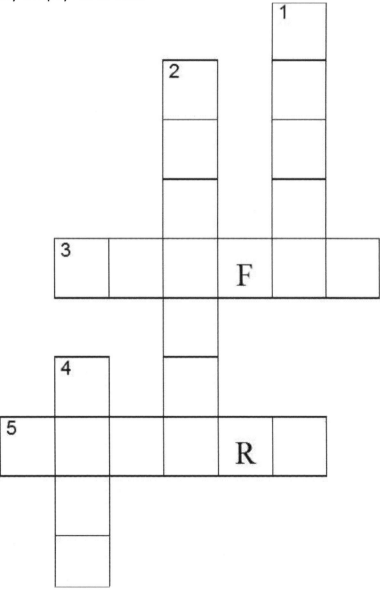

Day 35

Today you're going to draw a line through some more nouns. This time, every time you read a word that's a thing, draw a line through it. Choose a light color so you can still see the word. A thing might be something like a car, or it might be the name of a thing like Legos. Give it a try. It's okay if you miss one. It's also okay if you want to find people and places but pay special attention to things today.

A boy named Tom rode his bike down the street toward the school. He waved to his neighbor to say hello. His neighbor worked at Walmart but was home today. Then he saw the mailman coming. He raced home and asked his mom if he could wait by the mailbox.

Day 36

Trace and then write today's words.

daughter _____

beautiful _____

whomever _____

forever _____

_____

_____

_____

_____

Color in today's vocabulary word. Draw a picture to show its meaning. It means to struggle or fight vigorously or to make a great effort to achieve something. Here are some sentences that use the word.

I always strive to do my best.

It takes a brave person to strive against unjust laws.

Day 37

Trace and then write today's words.

inclination

regretted

faithfully

thoughts

Color in today's vocabulary word. Draw a picture to show its meaning. It means to be willing to do something wrong in order to get something for yourself. Here are some sentences that use the word.

The corrupt politician cheated to get more votes.

The corrupt salesman lied to sell the car.

Day 38

Trace and then write today's words.

violence

gopher

pitch

destroy

establish

Color in today's vocabulary word. Draw a picture to show its meaning. It means to create something intended to last. Here are some sentences that use the word.

I established Easy Peasy All-in-One Homeschool to help families continue homeschooling.

The no-texting-while-driving law was established to make the roads safer.

Day 39

Trace and then write today's words.

seven

alive

wives

hundredth

righteous

Color in today's vocabulary word. Draw a picture to show its meaning. It means to do what is right. Here are some sentences that use the word.

The Holy Spirit gives us the power to be righteous.

A righteous life is pleasing to the Lord.

Day 40

Trace and then write today's words.

He is faithful and
righteous to forgive
us our sins.

Today we're learning about floods. You could draw a picture of a flood. You could draw a picture of the Grand Canyon. You could draw a picture of a marine animal fossil. What do those have to do with floods?

Day 41

Trace and then write today's words.

decreased

mountains

subsided

recede

Color in today's vocabulary word. Draw a picture to show its meaning. It means to go back or gradually diminish. Here are some sentences that use the word.

The water receded after the flood.

He was growing bald as his hair receded with each passing year.

Day 42

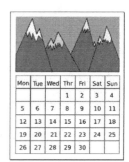

Trace and then write today's words.

abundantly

twenty-seventh

families

dried

Color in today's vocabulary word. Draw a picture to show its meaning. It means to lessen, reduce or remove. Here are some sentences that use the word.

His anger abated after I said I was sorry.

The rain abated in the evening.

Day 43

Trace and then write today's words.

require _____

account _____

cease _____

aroma _____

_____

_____

_____

_____

Color in today's vocabulary word. Draw a picture to show its meaning. It means purpose or what someone is determined to do. Here are some sentences that use the word.

I am intent on finishing the race even if I can't win.

He was intent on doing his best.

Day 44

Trace and then write today's words.

successive _____

generations _____

descendants _____

covenant _____

_____

_____

_____

successive

Color in today's vocabulary word. Draw a picture to show its meaning. It means coming after another. Here are some sentences that use the word.

For three successive years our family won the award.

Each successive book in the series was better than the one before.

Day 45

Trace and then write today's words.

The free gift of God is
eternal life in Christ
Jesus our Lord.

_____

_____

_____

_____

rainbows

Color in today's words. Your science lesson today is on rainbows and how dispersion separates light into colors. Can you draw a picture of it?

.

Day 46

Trace and then write today's words.

journeyed _____

scattered _____

thoroughly _____

building _____

_____

_____

_____

_____

Color in today's vocabulary word. Draw a picture to show its meaning.
Mortar is a mixture used to bind bricks or stones together. Here are some
sentences that use the word.

We mixed the mortar in the wheelbarrow before we took it to the
worksite.

We spread the mortar between the bricks to glue them into place.

Day 47

Trace and then write today's words.

possessions

pitched

acquired

Lot

accumulate

Color in today's vocabulary word. Draw a picture to show its meaning. It means to gather or to get more and more. Here are some sentences that use the word.

The snow accumulated until it reached the window.

He accumulated a large collection of bottle caps.

Day 48

Trace and then write today's words.

donkeys _____

woman _____

Egypt _____

escorted _____

_____

_____

_____

_____

severe

Color in today's vocabulary word. Draw a picture to show its meaning. It means intense or extreme. Here are some sentences that use the word.

The storm is severe.

He had a severe look on his face, and I knew I was in trouble.

Day 49

Trace and then write today's words.

formerly

belonged

number

exceedingly

Color in today's vocabulary word. Draw a picture to show its meaning. It means to support physically or mentally. Here are some sentences that use the word.

Our garden provided enough food to sustain us.

Reading my Bible every morning sustains me through the day.

Day 50

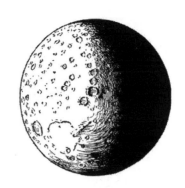

Trace and then write today's words.

God saw that the light was good.

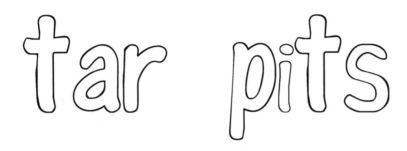

Color in today's words. Today's science lesson is on tar pits and quicksand. Can you draw a picture of today's lesson?

Day 51

Trace and then write today's words.

priest

sandal

enemies

except

Color in today's vocabulary word. Draw a picture to show its meaning. It means to dress someone in particular clothing or an ordered arrangement. Here are some sentences that use the word.

He was arrayed in a traditional Japanese kimono.

The hall was filled with a beautiful array of flowers.

Day 52

Trace and then write today's words.

heir

prey

pigeon

shield

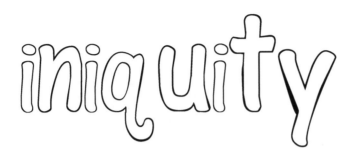

Color in today's vocabulary word. Draw a picture to show its meaning. It means sin. Here are some sentences that use the word.

When we confess our iniquities, God is faithful to forgive us.

King David's iniquity hurt all of Israel.

Day 53

Trace and then write today's words.

children _____

Egyptian _____

conceive _____

maid _____

_____

_____

_____

_____

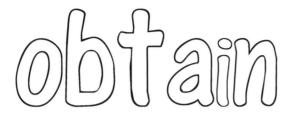

Color in today's vocabulary word. Draw a picture to show its meaning. It means to get or to acquire. Here are some sentences that use the word.

We were excited that we were able to obtain tickets to the show.

They obtained a valuable education at home.

Day 54

Trace and then write today's words.

authority _____

east _____

fleeing _____

against _____

_____

_____

_____

_____

affliction

Color in today's vocabulary word. Draw a picture to show its meaning. Affliction means pain and suffering. Here are some sentences that use the word.

The slave's affliction would have been unbearable without hope.

My affliction is small compared to Jesus' sacrifice for me.

Trace and then write today's words.

I will multiply your descendants as the stars of the heaven.

scientific notation

Color in today's word. Can you write a number in scientific notation?

Day 56

Trace and then write today's words.

throughout _____

foreigner _____

twelve _____

ninety-nine _____

_____

_____

_____

_____

Color in today's vocabulary word. Draw a picture to show its meaning. It means blocking something from getting to its intended destination. Here are some sentences that use the word.

The spy intercepted the letter intended for the general.

I intercepted him on his way out to look for you and let him know you were home.

Day 57

Trace and then write today's words.

appeared

opposite

bowed

measure

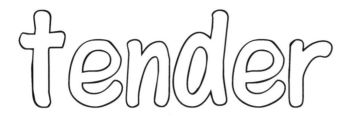

Color in today's vocabulary word. Draw a picture to show its meaning. It means easy to cut or chew. It can also mean gentle and kind. Here are some sentences that use the word.

He was tender toward his little sister when she got hurt.

This chicken is very tender and juicy.

Day 58

Trace and then write today's words.

denied

advanced

appointed

difficult

Color in today's vocabulary word. Draw a picture to show its meaning. It means designated, pre-arranged, or scheduled. Here are some sentences that use the word.

I was waiting for her at our appointed meeting time.

We set an appointed place where we would find each other after church.

Day 59

Trace and then write today's words.

righteous

command

judge

forty-five

Color in today's vocabulary word. Draw a picture to show its meaning. To venture means to undertake something risky or dangerous. Here are some sentences that use the word.

He ventured to attempt the half pipe for the first time.

I'm not willing to venture into the cave.

Day 60

Trace and then write today's words.

God called the light
day, and the darkness
He called night.

Color in today's word. Draw a picture to show the hanging gardens of Babylon.

Follow the maze and write each letter in order to make a word on each line. Can you find where one word ends and another begins?

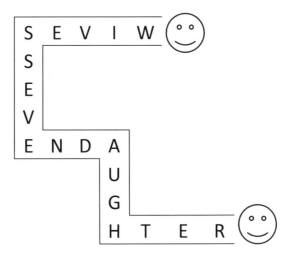

_____

_____

_____

Day 62

What does this crazy word say? It's two words mixed together. Write every other letter on a different line. Write the first letter on the top line and then the next letter on the bottom line. Write the next letter on the top line and the next letter write on the bottom line. Keep going to the end. What are the two words?

cchoinlcderievne

_____

_____

Day 63

Can you find the words? Draw a line between the letters to divide where one word ends and another begins.

Like this: end | begin

There are 6 words.

donkeyswomanshieldformbuildexceedingly

Directions:

This is like the game Battleship. I set this up so that you can play with a sibling using the Genesis Curriculum Workbook. On Day 65 you can do the same activity as in the Workbook as well.

Players write five words on their board, one letter per square. (I wrote in your words for you.) The words can go top to bottom and left to right. Words can intersect (share a letter, like in a crossword puzzle).

Players take turns guessing a square by naming its number and letter position. The other player must say either that it is blank or the letter in the square. If that square is blank, the player can place a dot or X in the square on the opponent's board to mark that it's been guessed already. If the square has a letter in it, the letter should be written in the square on the opponent's board.

You do not need to write on your board during the game. You just keep track of the game on the opponent's board. When you are asked about a square, you will check and tell what's in the square on the "My Ships" board.

The winner is the first to find all the letters of all five words on the opponent's board, in other words, to sink the opponent's word ships.

MY OPPONENT'S SHIPS

	1	2	3	4	5	6	7	8	9
A									
B									
C									
D									
E									
F									
G									
H									
I									

Day 45 words: decreased, mountains, subsided, recede, require, families, dried, cease, aroma, account, covenant

MY SHIPS

	1	2	3	4	5	6	7	8	9
A		R							C
B		E							E
C		Q							A
D		U		D	R	I	E	D	S
E		I							E
F		R		A	R	O	M	A	
G		E							
H		F	A	M	I	L	I	E	S
I									

Cut out the word strips and place them in a pile upside down. Choose someone to be the "spell checker." Take turns choosing a word from the pile and spelling it. Keep the word in front of you while you spell. You will stand and spell the word out loud. When you say a tall letter (t, h, f, d, b, l, k), reach both hands all the way up. When you say a hanging letter (y, p, g, j), touch your toes. Otherwise, put your hands on your hips.
(Parent note: You can print this out at genesiscurriculum.com if you don't want to cut your book. You can find it in the Workbook.)

throughout

foreigner

twelve

ninety-nine

appeared

opposite

bowed

denied

advanced

appointed

difficult

righteousness

command

judge

forty-five

Day 66

The Workbook activity today is charades. I thought you'd like to play too. I marked off what I thought were the easier ones to act out. Take turns choosing a word on the list to act out. You can also use the list to guess what words others are acting out.

strive - struggle

corrupt - willing to do something wrong

recede - to go back

venture - to do something daring

mortar - used to bind bricks

accumulate - gather

array - dress someone

iniquity - sin

affliction – suffering

tender - easy to chew

intercept - blocking something from getting to its intended destination

obtain - to get

****

abate - to lessen

intent - purpose

successive - coming after another

severe - intense

sustain - support

appointed - designated

establish - to create something

righteous - doing what is right

Day 67

Today you're going to draw a line through nouns again. Every time you read a word that's a person, draw a line through it. Choose a light color so you can still see the word. A person might be a name, like Peter, or it might be a person like a police officer or even just a baby. Is a baby a person? Yes! Give it a try. It's okay if you miss one. (A little note: Even though "he" and "she" are referring to people, we aren't going to put on line through those words.)

A young girl named Tabitha was watching her little brother. They lived in a white house on a quiet street, named Oak Lane. Their mother was taking care of the laundry. She was in the bedroom folding shirts and matching socks and putting them away. Their father had a job in an office. Tabitha was playing Peek-a-Boo. Her brother was just a baby, so he loved that game.

Day 68

Today you're going to draw a line through some more nouns. This time, every time you read a word that's a place, draw a line through it. Choose a light color so you can still see the word. A place might something like a church, or it might be the name of a place like Texas or Yellowstone National Park. Give it a try. It's okay if you miss one. It's also okay if you want to find the people again. Those are nouns and we're looking for nouns.

A young girl named Tabitha was watching her little brother. They lived in a white house on a quiet street, named Oak Lane. Their mother was taking care of the laundry. She was in the bedroom folding shirts and matching socks and putting them away. Their father had a job in an office. Tabitha was playing Peek-a-Boo. Her brother was just a baby, so he loved that game.

Day 69

Match the words to the definitions. In each group write number 1, 2 or 3 by the word that best fits the definition.

1. struggle

2. willing to do something wrong

3. doing what is right

___ righteous   ___ strive   ___ corrupt

1. to go back

2. used to bind bricks

3. gather

___ recede   ___ accumulate   ___ mortar

1. sin

2. to get

3. suffering

___ obtain   ___ iniquity   ___ affliction

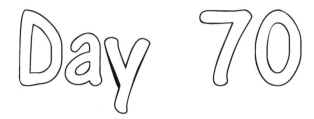

Day 70

Today you're going to draw a line through some more nouns. This time, every time you read a word that's a thing, draw a line through it. Choose a light color so you can still see the word. A thing might something like a bike, or it might be the name of a thing like Kleenex. Give it a try. It's okay if you miss one. It's also okay if you want to find the people and place nouns too, but pay special attention to the things.

A young girl named Tabitha was watching her little brother. They lived in a white house on a quiet street, named Oak Lane. Their mother was taking care of the laundry. She was in the bedroom folding shirts and matching socks and putting them away. Their father had a job in an office. Tabitha was playing Peek-a-Boo. Her brother was just a baby, so he loved that game.

Day 71

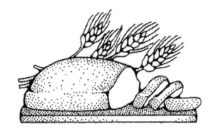

Trace and then write today's words.

inhabitants _____

surrounded _____

rained _____

urged _____

_____

_____

_____

_____

Color in today's vocabulary word. Draw a picture to show its meaning. It means to strongly persuade someone to do something. Here are some sentences that use the word.

I urge you to get your chores done quickly, so we can go outside to play.

He urged the crowd to form a line to get inside.

Day 72

Trace and then write today's words.

escape

punishment

dawn

seize

Color in today's vocabulary word. Draw a picture to show its meaning. It means to speak or act jokingly. Here are some sentences that use the word.

He jested that maybe I was really a fish since I liked swimming so much.

In jest he called my new hair cut weird.

Day 73

Trace and then write today's words.

pillar

toward

smoke

technique

Color in today's vocabulary word. Draw a picture to show its meaning. It means someone who lives in a place. Here are some sentences that use the word.

The birds are just a small portion of the inhabitants of the forest.

The inhabitants of this house have been away a long time. Look how long the grass has grown in their lawn.

Day 74

Trace and then write today's words.

ascend

preserve

remember

between

Color in today's vocabulary word. Draw a picture to show its meaning. It means to go up. Here are some sentences that use the word.

She ascended the mountain to the peak.

We ascended the many, many stairs to get to the top of the Statue of Liberty.

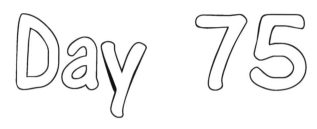

Trace and then write today's memory verse words.

As for me and my
house, we will serve
the Lord.

caves

We learned about caves. Can you draw a picture of the inside of a cave?

Day 76

Trace and then write today's words.

frightened _____

innocence _____

prophet _____

nation _____

_____

_____

_____

_____

Color in today's vocabulary word. Draw a picture to show its meaning. Integrity is the character quality of holding to strong moral principles. Here are some sentences that use the word.

His integrity kept him from keeping the money he found.

Because of his reputation for having integrity, people trusted him.

Trace and then write today's words.

womb

wander

thousand

pieces

vindication

Color in today's vocabulary word. Draw a picture to show its meaning. It means being shown innocent of an accusation of wrongdoing. Here are some sentences that use the word.

When they realized she hadn't even been at home, it was her vindication.

The perfect score on his retest was his vindication after being accused of cheating.

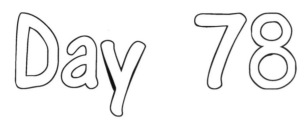 

Trace and then write today's words.

laughter

Isaac

weaned

bore

Color in today's vocabulary word. Draw a picture to show its meaning. It means to gradually get used to not having something you've become dependent on. Here are some sentences that use the word.

He weaned off the bottle and began using a cup.

She weaned herself off of TV, so she wouldn't waste so much time watching it.

Day 79

Trace and then write today's words.

Sarah

listen

die

angel

Color in today's vocabulary word. Draw a picture to show its meaning. It means extreme sorrow or worry or to cause extreme sorrow or worry. Here are some sentences that use the word.

I was distressed to find out we had a family of mice sharing our home with us.

The family was in distress after their home burned down.

Trace and then write today's words.

The Lord is not slow
about His promise.

Today's science lesson is on work. Can you draw a picture of work happening?

Day 81

Trace and then write today's words.

swear

therefore

falsely

any

Color in today's vocabulary word. Draw a picture to show its meaning. It means descendants of a person or all future generations. Here are some sentences that use the word.

My great-grandmother saved these letters for her posterity.

We buried a time capsule to save for posterity samples of life in the 20th century.

Day 82

Trace and then write today's words.

complain

oath

Philistine

ewe

seize

Color in today's vocabulary word. Draw a picture to show its meaning. It means to take hold of suddenly and forcibly. Here are some sentences that use the word.

The army seized the fortress.

I seized the flag and won the game for my team.

Day 83

Trace and then write today's words.

son

said

there

planted

Color in today's vocabulary word. Draw a picture to show its meaning. It means a gift or something offered. Here are some sentences that use the word.

I wanted to make up after our fight, so as an offering I brought a game for us to play together.

He slipped some money into an envelope and left it secretly on the desk as an offering for their missions work.

Day 84

Trace and then write today's words.

lamb _____

burnt _____

worship _____

knife _____

_____

_____

_____

_____

arose

Color in today's vocabulary word. Draw a picture to show its meaning. It means to stand up or to emerge. Here are some sentences that use the word.

A problem arose with the pies.

He arose from his seat on the platform and everyone grew quiet.

Day 85

Trace and then write today's words.

As for me, I know that
my Redeemer lives.

Color in today's word. Can you draw a picture of a fire? Fires give off heat. When two elements combine together and give heat, we call that an exothermic reaction.

Day 86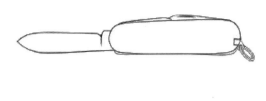

Trace and then write today's words.

two

stretch

wood

technology

Color in today's vocabulary word. Draw a picture to show its meaning. It means an elevated surface where religious rites are performed. Here are some sentences that use the word.

They stood before the altar to take their wedding vows.

The Israelites built an altar to offer a sacrifice to God.

Day 87

Trace and then write today's words.

thicket

caught

provide

mount

Color in today's vocabulary word. Draw a picture to show its meaning. It means a dense group of shrubs, bushes, or small trees. Here are some sentences that use the word.

Our ball got caught in the thicket, and we couldn't get it out without getting poked.

Some small animals stay safe by living in the thicket where bigger animals can't get to them.

Day 88

Trace and then write today's words.

declare _____

Abraham _____

second _____

seashore _____

_____

_____

_____

_____

declare

Color in today's vocabulary word. Draw a picture to show its meaning. It means to state clearly or to make known publicly. Here are some sentences that use the word.

The candidate declared he would make the best president.

My brother declared that anyone who touched his model car would be in trouble.

Day 89

Trace and then write today's words.

eight

children

sensational

tremendous

omniscient

Color in today's vocabulary word. Draw a picture to show its meaning. It means all-knowing. Here are some sentences that use the word.

I don't know the future; only God is omniscient.

We can never hide anything from our omniscient mother.

Trace and then write today's memory verse words.

By faith Abraham received the promises.

I think you might like to do Science Review 9.

Circle one option from each set of choices. It's best to choose different options for each dog. After you make your choices, you can draw a picture of each if you like.

MOM DOG:
Hair: long or short
Body: big or small or medium
Legs: long or short
Ears: long or short
Coat: solid or spotted
Color: brown or white or black

DAD DOG:
Hair: long or short
Body: big or small or medium
Legs: long or short
Ears: long or short
Coat: solid or spotted
Color: brown or white or black

For each trait, circle either odd or even.

Hair: odd/even   Ears: odd/even   Body: odd/even
Legs: odd/even   Coat: odd/even   Color: odd/even

Now, build your baby dog. Ask your parent to read you the rest of the instructions.

Hair: long or short

Body: big or small or medium

Legs: long or short

Ears: long or short

Coat: solid or spotted

Color: brown or white or black

Day 91

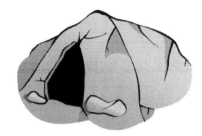

Trace and then write today's words.

mourn

burial

burying

approach

mourn

Color in today's vocabulary word. Draw a picture to show its meaning. It means to feel deeply saddened about a loss. Here are some sentences that use the word.

He mourned for a week after his cat died.

They were mourning the loss of their house after the fire but were grateful they were all safe.

Day 92

Trace and then write today's words.

sight _____

answers _____

price _____

people _____

_____

_____

_____

approach

Color in today's vocabulary word. Draw a picture to show its meaning. It means to come near or to speak to someone about something for the first time. Here are some sentences that use the word.

She approached the deer very slowly so that it wouldn't get scared away.

They approached me with the idea of forming a chess club.

Day 93

Trace and then write today's words.

worth

four

weigh

confines

commercial

Color in today's vocabulary word. Draw a picture to show its meaning. It means intended for profit. Here are some sentences that use the word.

It seems most people do things for commercial gain.

Are you going to start a commercial business or a non-profit organization?

Day 94

Trace and then write today's words.

hundred

commercial

standard

satisfied

standard

Color in today's vocabulary word. Draw a picture to show its meaning. It means to be accepted as normal or something used as a measure to compare other things against. Here are some sentences that use the word.

This is the standard way to do this kind of math problem.

This isn't up to her high standard of cleanliness.

Trace and then write your memory verse words.

Jesus said to her,
"I am the resurrection
and the life."

_____

_____

_____

_____

We are learning today about the mantle. It's under the crust of the earth. It's made of melty rock. Can you draw a picture of the inside of the earth?

Find the words below in the puzzle below. The words are written across like regular words except for one that goes down.

ALIEN   DAWN SEIZE   URGED

```
A   L   I   E   N   D
D   W   E   R   O   I
A   R   Q   E   Z   P
W   S   E   I   Z   E
N   W   T   U   T   I
W   U   R   G   E   D
```

Use the clues to fill in the missing letters and then the same letter in the blank with the matching number. What is the mystery word?

___ i s ___ e n
 1   2

___ a u g h t e r   what comes out when you laugh
 1

p r o p h e ___   someone who speaks for God
          2

Directions:

This is like the game Battleship. I set this up so that you can play with a sibling using the Genesis Curriculum Workbook.

Players write seven words on their board, one letter per square. (I wrote in your words for you.) The words can go top to bottom and left to right. Words can intersect (share a letter, like in a crossword puzzle).

Players take turns guessing a square by naming its number and letter position. The other player must say either that it is blank or the letter in the square. If that square is blank, the player can place a dot or X in the square on the opponent's board to mark that it's been guessed already. If the square has a letter in it, the letter should be written in the square on the opponent's board.

You do not need to write on your board during the game. You just keep track of the game on the opponent's board. When you are asked about a square, you will check and tell what's in the square on the "My Ships" board.

The winner is the first to find all the letters of all five words on the opponent's board, in other words, to sink the opponent's word ships.

MY OPPONENT'S SHIPS

	1	2	3	4	5	6	7	8	9
A									
B									
C									
D									
E									
F									
G									
H									
I									

Day 85: swear, falsely, army, ewe, complain, oath, son, said, there, lamb, burnt, worship, knife

MY SHIPS

	1	2	3	4	5	6	7	8	9
A	K	N	I	F	E				C
B									O
C		T		S	O	N			M
D		H							P
E		E							L
F		R		L	A	M	B		A
G		E							I
H		F	A	L	S	E	L	Y	N
I									

Can you use the letters below to put the correct first letter on each word?

P S A

___econd

___rovide

___gainst

Find your way from the top left to the bottom right of the maze.

START

Maze made at: http://gwydir.demon.co.uk/jo/maze/makemaze/index.htm

Day 101

Give the appropriate type of word for each blank. You might want to have someone else write in the word for you. Then read the story with your words inserted. This is like Mad Libs. (This activity is in the Genesis Curriculum Workbook – The Book of Genesis.)

_____ 1. adjective (a word that describes how something looks or feels)

_____ 2. action verb (something people do, example: run)

_____ 3. same verb in the past tense (write it like it happened yesterday)

_____ 4. adjective (a word like fast, slow, easy, hard, interesting, boring)

_____ 5. plural noun (plural means more than one, like apples, with an S)

_____ 6. possessive adjective (one of these: my, your, its, our, their)

_____ 7. a color

_____ 8. noun (person, place or thing)

_____ 9. adjective (a word that describes how something looks or feels)

_____ 10. noun (person, place or thing)

_____ 11. action verb in the past tense

_____ 12. body part

_____ 13. noun, used for action in number 2 (ex. run, sneakers)

_____ 14. noun

_____ 15. number

_____ 16. length of time

_____ 17. action verb, past tense

_____18. adjective

_____19. noun, common noun for who does action in number 2
                  (example: runs, runner)

_____20. proper noun, name of someone who does the action in #2

This is the paragraph that you will use with your words. Don't look at this until you have finished filling in your blanks on Grammar Review 6.

I had a 1. _____ idea.

I was going to 2. _____.

I never 3. _____ before, but I had seen it on the Olympics, and it looked 4. _____.

I got my 5. _____ together and headed out the door. I ran down the street to 6. _____ 7. _____ 8. _____.

It had a 9. _____ 10. _____.

I 11. _____ my 12. _____ firmly on my 13. _____ and took off down the 14. _____.

It lasted about 15. _____ 16. _____.

I 17. _____.

I was not as 18. _____ as the 19. _____ on TV like 20. _____.

Day 102

Circle the letter of the word that best matches the definition.

1. the character quality of holding to strong moral principles
A.   seize
B.   accuse
C.   jest
D.   integrity

2. to speak or act jokingly
A.   seize
B.   jest
C.   declare
D.   integrity

3. to take hold of suddenly and forcibly
A.   altar
B.   seize
C.   declare
D.   mourn

4. to state clearly, to make known publicly
A.   declare
B.   integrity
C.   posterity
D.   mourn

5. to feel deeply saddened over a loss
A.   jest
B.   altar
C.   wean
D.   mourn

6. to go up
A.   integrity
B.   ascend
C.   mourn
D.   descend

Day 103

Find the action verbs. Verbs are things people do. They don't have to be running and jumping to be action verbs. Thinking and sleeping are action verbs too even though you may not be moving when you are doing them. They are things people do. Try to find at least one action verb in each sentence (some have more than one) and draw a line under it or through it with a light color so that you can still see the words. It's okay if you miss some.

I like to run. I run with my dog every day. He likes to go outside. We sometimes go to the park and play. He chases squirrels. I read. We both drink some water from the fountains before we go home.

This paragraph is all mixed up. Can you put the vocabulary words in their correct places?

We were <u>distressed</u> to sign up for this field trip. We were getting a free tour of the colonial house. As we <u>urged</u> the property, we passed a thicket. We were <u>approached</u> to learn that the colonial house needed urgent repairs. We were happy to give a donation to help them.

We were _____ to sign up for this field trip. We were

getting a free tour of the colonial house. As we _____

the property, we passed a thicket. We were _____ to

learn that the colonial house needed urgent repairs. We were happy to

give a donation to help them.

Day 105

Find the action verbs. Verbs are things people do. They don't have to be running and jumping to be action verbs. Thinking and sleeping are action verbs too even though you may not be moving when you are doing them. They are things people do. Try to find at least one action verb in each sentence (some have more than one) and draw a line under it or through it with a light color so that you can still see the words. It's okay if you miss some.

My friend Sarah likes to come over to my house to play. We lay in the grass and watch the clouds. Once we saw one cloud that she thought looked like a turtle, but I thought that it looked like a snail. Did you know that clouds are made of water? There in the sky they float along as the wind pushes them. She and I also make lemonade. We squeeze the lemons, add water and sugar, and stir.

Day 106

Trace and then write today's spelling words.

age

thigh

beware

concern

concerning

Color in today's vocabulary word. Draw a picture to show its meaning. It means about, related to a subject. Here are some sentences that use the word.

If you have any information concerning the damage to the school, please contact the police.

I need to speak with you concerning this letter I just received.

Day 107

Trace and then write today's spelling words.

quickly

lower

shoulder

emptied

Today's word is adverb. It's the kind of word that is mostly used to describe nouns. A lot of times adverbs end in -LY.

In the sentences below, underline all of the words that end in -LY.

1. He hastily does his chores because he eagerly wants to get to play.

   o Did you underline the LY adverbs in that sentence?
   - What does hastily describe?
     - how he does his chores
   - What does eagerly describe?
     - how he wants to go play

2. Thankfully I was able to nimbly free myself.

3. Samuel was playfully teasing the dog by quickly making a throwing motion and then immediately hiding the ball.

Day 108

Trace and then write today's words.

camel

lodge

bracelet

guide

Color in today's vocabulary word. Draw a picture to show its meaning. It means to stay a short time in a place such as a home or hotel. It could also mean to become stuck in something. Here are some sentences that use the word.

He decided to lodge with their family until the blizzard passed and the roads were cleared.

I had a piece of food lodged in between my teeth.

Day 109

Trace and then write today's words.

business

successful

blessed

down

adverbs

We're going to look at adverbs in today's reading.

Here are some phrases from today's reading. Find the -LY adverb or adverbs in each that tell us more about the verb.

- the Lord has greatly blessed
- deal kindly and truly

The first example tells us how God blessed, greatly.
The second example tells how they are going to deal with him, kindly and truly.

Underline the adverbs in the sentence below.

He slowly made his way across the room to dutifully clean up the mess.

Day 110

Trace and then write your memory verse words.

The Lord is the one who
goes ahead of you.
Do not fear.

_____

_____

_____

_____

George Washington Carver

What would be a good picture for this great man of God?

Day 111

Trace and then write today's spelling words.

grief

envied

defiance

thirty-seven

Color in today's vocabulary word. Draw a picture to show its meaning. It means to be upset over what someone else has that you don't. Here are some sentences that use the word.

She envied her sister's long hair.

Be grateful for everything so that you don't envy what others have.

Day 112

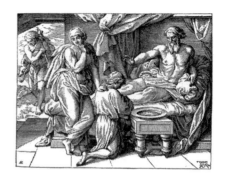

Trace and then write today's spelling words.

descend

console

deceitful

violently

deceive

Color in today's vocabulary word. Draw a picture to show its meaning. It means to lie or to trick someone. Here are some sentences that use the word.

He tried to deceive his mother by hiding his broccoli under the table.

You can't deceive God because He sees everything.

Day 113

Trace and then write today's spelling words.

flock _____

almond _____

continue _____

distance _____

_____

_____

_____

_____

Color in today's vocabulary word. Draw a picture to show its meaning. It means weak. Here are some sentences that use the word.

The feeble old chair wasn't strong enough to hold me.

He made a feeble attempt at getting the yard picked up before declaring it was too hard.

Day 114

Trace and then write today's spelling words.

embrace _____

gracious _____

prevail _____

wrestle _____

_____

_____

_____

_____

Color in today's vocabulary word. Draw a picture to show its meaning. It means to win. Here are some sentences that use the word.

We prevailed in getting the puzzle completed in one day.

The Israelites prevailed over their enemies when they obeyed God.

Day 115

Trace and then write today's memory verse words.

For I know the plans I
have for you.
Plans to give you hope
and a future.

_____

_____

_____

_____

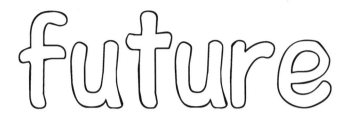

No science lesson today. What do you think your future will look like? Draw a picture of it.

Day 116

Trace and then write today's spelling words.

bind _____

erect _____

rebuke _____

jealous _____

_____

_____

_____

Color in today's vocabulary word. Draw a picture to show its meaning. It means to scold, to tell someone their behavior is wrong in a sharp manner. Here are some sentences that use the word.

I had to rebuke him for disobeying.

We were rebuked when we kicked the ball over the fence.

Day 117

Trace and then write today's spelling words.

pasture

pasturing

welfare

devour

devour

Color in today's vocabulary word. Draw a picture to show its meaning. It means to eat up hungrily or to destroy completely. Here are some sentences that use the word.

He devoured the piece of apple pie.

The boll weevil devoured the cotton crop.

Day 118

Trace and then write today's spelling words.

rescue

further

balm

stripped

Color in today's vocabulary word. Draw a picture to show its meaning. It means a cream used for medicine, a sweet smell, or anything that heals or soothes. Here are some sentences that use the word.

I made up a balm of baking soda and water to rub onto her bee sting.

The music is a balm to my fussy baby, always calming him down.

Day 119

Trace and then write today's spelling words.

aromatic _____

myrrh _____

Joseph _____

caravan _____

_____

_____

_____

_____

Color in today's vocabulary word. Draw a picture to show its meaning. It means to get a benefit, or it can refer to money gained. Here are some sentences that use the word.

He made a profit from his lemonade stand.

I really profited from the sermon this week; I learned a lot of new things.

Day 120

Trace and then write today's memory verse words.

God causes all things
to work together for
good to those who
love God.

shadow effect

Color in today's words. Can you draw a picture of it? It's when a mountain forces air to rise making the air cool and causing it to rain.

Day 121

Trace and then write today's spelling words.

officer

desire

handsome

appearance

prosper

Color in today's vocabulary word. Draw a picture to show its meaning. It means to succeed financially or physically. Here are some sentences that use the word.

Joseph prospered in everything he did.

Our business prospered after we advertised our services.

Day 122

Trace and then write today's spelling words.

garment

Hebrew

screamed

fled

garment

Color in today's vocabulary word. Draw a picture to show its meaning. It means a piece of clothing. Here are some sentences that use the word.

He hung the garment carefully to keep it from wrinkling.

Joseph's gift of a special garment made his brothers jealous.

Day 123

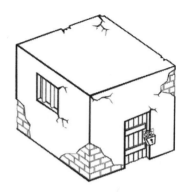

Trace and then write today's words.

jailer

extend

charge

anger

supervise

Color in today's vocabulary word. Draw a picture to show its meaning. It means to keep watch over someone while they work. Here are some sentences that use the word.

Joseph didn't have to be supervised because he was trustworthy and responsible.

I supervise my little brothers playing in our back yard.

Day 124

Trace and then write today's words.

furious

officials

baker

confinement

Color in today's vocabulary word. Draw a picture to show its meaning. It means to put restrictions on someone or something. Here are some sentences that use the word.

I felt confined in the small space.

We confined our rabbit to the deck so that he wouldn't escape.

Day 125

Trace and then write your memory verse words.

But to do justice, to love kindness, and to walk humbly with your God.

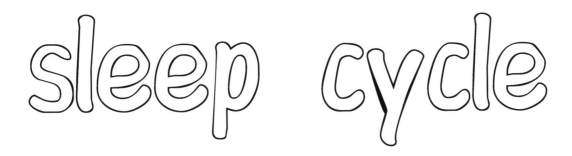

sleep cycle

Today you are learning about sleep. Draw a picture of someone sleeping and dreaming. What's the dream?

Day 126

Trace and then write today's spelling words.

sorts

basket

favorably

chief

interpretation

Color in today's vocabulary word. Draw a picture to show its meaning. An interpretation is the explanation of something's meaning. Here are some sentences that use the word.

Joseph gave Pharaoh the interpretation of his dream.

I had to ask for an interpretation because I couldn't understand Hungarian.

Day 127

Trace and then write today's spelling words.

scorch _____

captain _____

stalk _____

magician _____

_____

_____

_____

_____

Color in today's vocabulary word. Draw a picture to show its meaning. It means scrawny looking, especially looking thin from hunger. Here are some sentences that use the word.

She looked gaunt after two weeks in the jungle.

The children were gaunt after their long walk to the refugee camp.

Day 128

Trace and then write today's words.

subsequent

famine

unknown

abundance

subsequent

Color in today's vocabulary word. Draw a picture to show its meaning. It means coming after something, following. Here are some sentences that use the word.

Each subsequent book in the series was better than the one before.

I hope that you are going to be on time for our subsequent meetings.

Day 129

Trace and then write today's words.

proposal

exact

discern

inform

discern

Color in today's vocabulary word. Draw a picture to show its meaning. It means to be able to recognize or to see something and distinguish what it is. Here are some sentences that use the word.

Through the fog it was hard to discern if we were at the right street.

We can ask God for wisdom to discern what is truly of Him.

Day 130

Trace and then write your memory verse.

Cast your burden upon the Lord and He will sustain you.

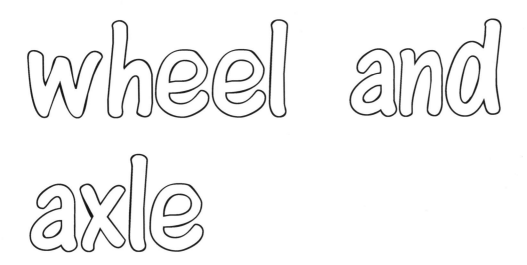

wheel and axle

Today we are talking about wheel and axle vehicles. Can you draw a picture of a vehicle that uses wheels and axles?

Follow the maze and write each letter in order to make a word on each line.
Can you find where one word ends and another begins?

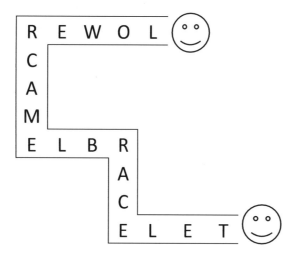

_____

_____

_____

Day 132

The beginnings and ends of the words have been mixed up! Can you put the words back in order? Cut out the word parts and rearrange them or write the real words on the lines. (Parent note: If you want to cut these out but not cut your book, come to genesiscurriculum.com to print this page.)

_____

_____

Day 133

Directions:

This is like the game Battleship. I set this up so that you can play with a sibling using the Genesis Curriculum Workbook.

Players write six words on their board, one letter per square. (I wrote in your words for you.) The words can go top to bottom and left to right. Words can intersect (share a letter, like in a crossword puzzle).

Players take turns guessing a square by naming its number and letter position. The other player must say either that it is blank or the letter in the square. If that square is blank, the player can place a dot or X in the square on the opponent's board to mark that it's been guessed already. If the square has a letter in it, the letter should be written in the square on the opponent's board.

You do not need to write on your board during the game. You just keep track of the game on the opponent's board. When you are asked about a square, you will check and tell what's in the square on the "My Ships" board.

The winner is the first to find all the letters of all five words on the opponent's board, in other words, to sink the opponent's word ships.

MY OPPONENT'S SHIPS

	1	2	3	4	5	6	7	8	9
A									
B									
C									
D									
E									
F									
G									
H									
I									

Day 85: swear, falsely, army, ewe, complain, oath, son, said, there, lamb, burnt, worship, knife

MY SHIPS

	1	2	3	4	5	6	7	8	9
A		S	W	E	A	R			
B				K	N	I	F		E
C		S							B
D		O							U
E		N							R
F			A	R	M	Y			N
G									T
H		C	O	M	P	L	A	I	N
I						O	A	T	H

Day 134

This activity is in the GC – Book of Genesis Workbook as well. Cut out the word strips and place them in a pile upside down. Choose someone to be the "spell checker." Take turns choosing a word from the pile and spelling it. Keep the word in front of you while you spell. You will stand and spell the word out loud. When you say a tall letter (t, h, f, d, b, l, k), reach both hands all the way up. When you say a hanging letter (y, p, g, j), touch your toes. Otherwise, put your hands on your hips. (Parent note: You can print this out at genesiscurriculum.com if you don't want to cut your book.)

officer

desire

appearance

handsome

garment

Hebrew

fled

jailer

extend

charge

anger

furious

officials

baker

confinement

Day 135

On each row the two words are missing the same last letter. Can you figure out what's missing?

unknow___   discer___

captai___   magicia___

Day 136

Find the action verbs. Verbs are things people do. They don't have to be running and jumping to be action verbs. Thinking and sleeping are action verbs too. They are things people do. It's okay if you miss some. Try to find at least one action verb in each sentence (some have more than one) and draw a line under it or through it with a light color so that you can still see the words.

We walked to the sunny park today. I climbed up the slippery slides and slid down. We raced to see who was fastest. We swung on the plastic swings. We practiced our soccer skills and threw and caught soft balls. We picnicked in the green grass when we were done.

Day 137

This activity is in the Workbook as well. Choose a word to either act out or to draw. Take turns at guessing.

concerning – related to a subject

adverb – word that describes how something is done

lodge – to stay a short time in a place such as a home or hotel

envy – jealousy; being upset over what someone else has

deceit – the act of lying

feeble – weak

droves – a large crowd

prevail – to win, to be widespread or more frequently occurring

rebuke – to scold; to sharply tell someone their behavior is wrong

devour – to eat up hungrily; to beat or destroy completely

balm – cream used for medicine, or anything that heals or soothes

profit – get a benefit, often refers to money

prosper – to succeed financially or physically

garment – a piece of clothing

supervise – to keep watch over someone while they work

confine – to place restrictions on someone or something

interpretation – the explanation of something's meaning

gaunt – scrawny looking, especially looking thin from hunger

subsequent – coming after something, following

discern – to be able to recognize something and distinguish what it is

Day 138

Find the nouns. Nouns are people, places and things. There are no people in this one. I don't name people. I use words like We and I in the place of naming the people. Don't mark those words. Look for five things and one place.

We walked to the sunny park today. I climbed up the

slippery slides and slid down. We raced to see who was

fastest. We swung on the plastic swings. We practiced

our soccer skills and threw and caught soft balls. We

picnicked in the green grass when we were done.

Day 139

Draw a line matching the words to their definitions.

to eat up hungrily

weak

a piece of clothing

scrawny looking

to win

garment

feeble

devour

prevail

gaunt

Day 140

Find the nouns again. There were five things and one place. The hardest was the word "skills." They are a thing. There were six nouns and there are six adjectives. There is one adjective in front of each noun. That means there are six adjectives. Adjectives describe nouns. Circle the six adjectives. They are the words right in front of the nouns that describe them.

We walked to the sunny park today. I climbed up the

slippery slides and slid down. We raced to see who was

fastest. We swung on the plastic swings. We practiced

our soccer skills and threw and caught soft balls. We

picnicked in the green grass when we were done.

Thank you for using the Genesis Curriculum.

Genesis Curriculum takes a book of the Bible and turns it into daily lessons in science, social studies, and language arts. Daily lessons also include reading a portion from the Bible, practicing a weekly memory verse, discussing a thought-provoking question, and learning a Biblical language.

Genesis Curriculum also offers:

GC Steps: This is GC's preschool and kindergarten curriculum. There are three years (ages three through six) where kids will learn to read and write as well as develop beginning math skills.

A Mind for Math: This is GC's elementary school learning-together math program based on the curriculum's daily Bible reading. Children work together as well as have their own leveled workbook.

Rainbow Readers: These are leveled reading books. They each have a unique dictionary with the included words underlined in the text. They are also updated to use modern American spelling.

GenesisCurriculum.com

Made in the USA
Coppell, TX
26 August 2020